Contents

Map of the Book

Title	Function	Text Type and Writing Skill	Review Focus	Grammar	Vocabulary
UNIT 1 New Kids in Class pages 4–5	Introducing yourself	**Dialogue** Text-building: *I, he, she; my*	Capital letters	Present simple: *be*	Real and imaginary creatures
UNIT 2 Sea School pages 6–7	Identifying objects	**Poem** Text-building: questions and answers	Presentation	Present simple: *be* affirmative / questions	Classroom objects
UNIT 3 Funny Family pages 8–9	Describing a family	**Composition** Text-building: *he, she*	Possessive apostrophe Pronouns	Present simple: *be, like*	Family Interests
UNIT 4 Space Town pages 10–11	Describing a town	**Composition** Text-building: *it*	Missing words: indefinite article	*There is / are*	Urban environment
UNIT 5 Saturday with Lizzy and Larry pages 14–15	Narrating daily routines	**Composition** Text-building: *before / after*; pronouns Free writing	Checking grammar	Present simple 1st / 3rd person: affirmative / negative	Times of day Leisure activities
UNIT 6 The Count's Kitchen pages 16–17	Describing a room	**Poem** Text-building: *and*	Tidy lines and margins	*There is / are a / some*	Food Animals
UNIT 7 The Haunted Holiday Home pages 18–19	Giving instructions	**Warning notice** Text-building: *but*	Spelling	Imperatives: affirmative / negative	Household objects and associated verbs Adjectives
UNIT 8 Two Bedrooms pages 20–21	Describing where things are	**Composition** Text-building: possessive adjectives Free writing	Missing words	Prepositions of place	Parts of a room Personal belongings

Title	Function	Text Type and Writing Skill	Review Focus	Grammar	Vocabulary
UNIT 9 **The Alien of Planet Zeta** pages 24–25	Describing appearances and habits	**Report with headings** Text-building: *and, with*	Apostrophe Handwriting	Present simple: *has got, plays, drives, rides*	Parts of the body Hobbies
UNIT 10 **Jane Bond Goes to Seal Island** pages 26–27	Telling an adventure story	**Film review** Text-building: pronouns; combining sentences with *and*	Neat editing Subject and object pronouns	Present simple: 3rd person Subject / object pronouns	Action verbs Forms of transport Classifying
UNIT 11 **My Friend Lucy** pages 28–29	Identifying people in a picture	**Informal letter** Text-building: prepositional clauses	Adding detail	Present continuous	Clothing Colours
UNIT 12 **Robodog** pages 30–31	Describing abilities	**Advert** Text-building: listing; commas; *and, also*	Punctuation	*Can / can't* for ability	Work and leisure activities Classifying
UNIT 13 **Homeland** pages 34–35	Describing where you live	**Composition** Free writing	Word order	Adverbs of frequency Pronouns *it / there*	Landscape Weather
UNIT 14 **Two Days at Adventure World** pages 36–37	Describing an itinerary	**Postcard** Text-building: sequencing	Sequencing words	Present continuous: future	Adventure Sequencing words
UNIT 15 **Animal Hotel** pages 38–39	Describing a busy scene	**Monologue** Writing from the reader's point of view	Checking grammar	*Going to* future	Animals Activities
UNIT 16 **What a Strange Night!** pages 40–41	Narrating a story	**Composition** Text-building: *and, with* Free writing	Handwriting Spelling Grammar Punctuation	Past simple: *was / were*	Descriptive adjectives Classifying

New Kids in Class

Introducing yourself

Words

1   Choose names, ages and places for the new students in the picture on the
    opposite page. You can use words from the boxes. Complete the table.

Names   Baboo   Cheltin   Moog   Oscar
Paul   Tex   Tilda   Zildra

How old   2 years old   8 years old
9 years old   12 years old   59 years old
302 years old

Where from   Africa   Amazonia
England   Hollywood   Mars   Saturn

	Name	How old	Where from
Monster	Grostick	201 years old	Redistan
Alien			
Animal			
Robot	D2XYZ	1 year old	Antarctica
Person			

Sentences

2   Answer these questions for Grostick.

Hello. What's your name?

_____

How old are you, Grostick?

_____

Where are you from?

_____

And who is this?
This is my friend D2XYZ.
How old is she?

_____

Where is she from?

_____

Writing

3   Read this paragraph by Grostick. Then
    write a paragraph for one of the other
    new students.

> Hello. My name is Grostick. I'm
> 201 years old. I'm from Redistan.
> My friend's name is D2XYZ. She's
> 1 year old. She's from Antarctica.

4   Review your writing. Follow this track.

Sea School

Identifying objects

Words

1 Underline the things in your classroom.

> bag ~~bin~~ blackboard book chair
> computer ~~desk~~ ~~door~~ ~~file~~ ~~map~~
> notebook pen ~~pencil~~ pencil case
> piece of paper poster ruler table
> ~~TV~~ video wall

2 Write two more words under each shape.

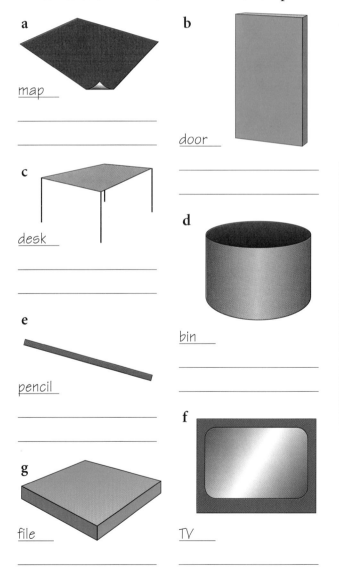

a
map
_____
_____

b
door
_____
_____

c
desk
_____
_____

d
bin
_____
_____

e
pencil
_____
_____

f
TV
_____
_____

g
file
_____
_____

Sentences

3 Read about this object.

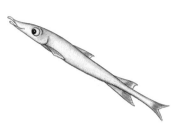

What's this?

Is it a ruler?

Is it a pencil?

No, it's a pen!

4 Write about this object.

_____?

_____video?

_____TV?

_____!

> ### Writing

5 Write a poem called *Sea School*. Draw
pictures. Use this beginning. Choose three
more groups of words from Activity 2.

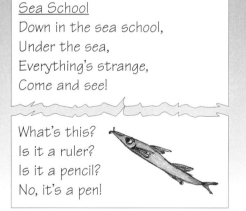

> Sea School
> Down in the sea school,
> Under the sea,
> Everything's strange,
> Come and see!

> What's this?
> Is it a ruler?
> Is it a pencil?
> No, it's a pen!

6 Review your writing. Follow this track.

Funny Family

Describing a family

Words

1 This is Jenny. Find her family in the picture on the opposite page. Match the people with these hobbies.

| art football hamburgers music |
| pop magazines science swimming |

a mother   _art_____

b father   _____

c big brother _____

d baby brother _____

e little sister _____

f grandmother _____

g grandfather _____

Sentences

2 Give names to the people in Jenny's family. Write the names on this family tree.

3 This is what Jenny wrote about her family. Write their names. Then write sentences about their hobbies.

a My mother's name is _____ .
   _She likes art ._____

b My father's name is _____ .
   _____

c My big brother's name is_____ .
   _____

d My baby brother's name is_____ .
   _____

e My little sister's name is _____ .
   _____

f My grandmother's name is _____ .
   _____

g My grandfather's name is _____ .
   _____

Writing

4 Write about your family. Begin like this:

My name is _____ . I'm _____
years old. I like _____ . My
_____'s name is …

5 Review your writing. Follow this track.

Jenny

SPACE TOWN

Picture A

Picture B

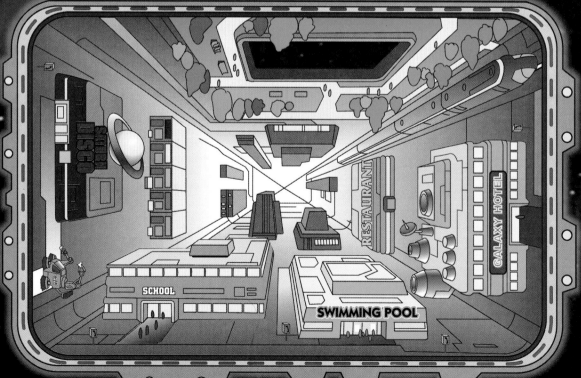

Describing a town

Words

1 Look at the pictures on the opposite page.
Write these words in the table.

| ~~bus~~ ~~café~~ cinema disco post boxes restaurant shops sports centre supermarket swimming pool telephone boxes train |

_____
_____

Picture A	Picture B
bus	
café	

_____
_____

Sentences

2 Look at the pictures on the opposite page.
Write sentences about these things.

_____
_____

There is a cinema in
Picture A.

_____
_____

_____
_____

There are telephone
boxes in Picture B.

_____
_____

_____
_____

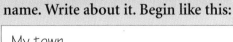

Writing

3 Choose Picture A or B. Give the town a
name. Write about it. Begin like this:

My town
I live in _____ . It is a
nice town. There are trees and a park.
There is a school and a hotel.

4 Review your writing. Follow this track.

Review Your Writing

UNIT 1

1 Read this piece of writing. Correct the mistakes.

> my name is Baboo. i'm 12 years old. I'm from amazonia. my
>
> friend's name is oscar. he's 9 years old. he's from England.

2 You are the teacher. Give the writing a mark for capital letters.

Grammar =   10/10
Spelling =   10/10
Capital letters =   /10

3 Look at your writing. Give your writing a mark for capital letters.

Finished? Find a pencil in the picture on page 4!

UNIT 2

1 Read these two poems. Are they nice? Draw one of these next to each poem.

> What's this?
> Is it a ruler?
> Is it a pencil?
> No, it's a pen!
>
> What's this?
> Is it a video?
> Is it a TV?
> No, it's a computer!

> What's this?
> Is it a ruler?
> Is it a pencil?
> No, it's a pen!
>
> What's this?
> Is it a video?
> Is it a TV?
> No, it's a computer!

2 Look at your poem. Is it nice? Draw one of these next to your poem.

Finished? Find this in the picture on page 6!

UNIT 3

1 Read these pieces of writing. Correct the mistakes.

> My mothers name is Anna. She likes art. My fathers name is Tony. He likes pop magazines.

> My mother's name is Anna. He likes art. My father's name is Tony. She likes pop magazines.

2 Write one of these comments next to each piece of writing.

a Be careful:
girl = she
boy = he

b Remember the **'** .

3 Read your writing. Check *she*, *he* and **'** .

Finished? How many hands can you find in the picture on page 8?

UNIT 4

1 Look at this piece of writing. There are missing words. Write the missing words.

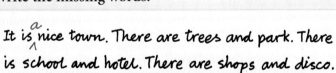

> It is ^a^ nice town. There are trees and park. There is school and hotel. There are shops and disco.

2 Read your writing. Are there missing words? Write the words now.

Finished? Are there more post boxes or more telephone boxes in the pictures on page 10?

Saturday with Lizzy and Larry

7.30

before breakfast

after breakfast

in the afternoon

before bed

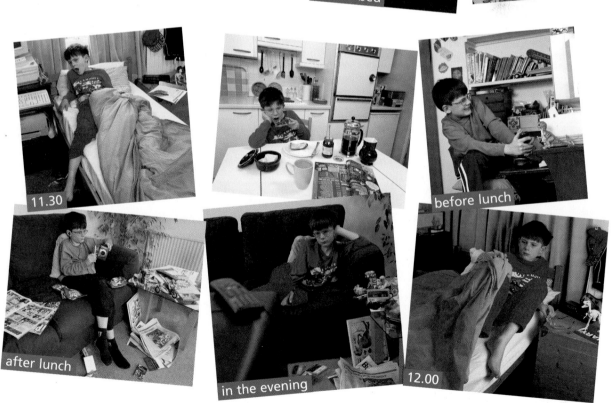

11.30

before lunch

after lunch

in the evening

12.00

14

Narrating daily routines

Words

1 Put these pieces together to make times of day.

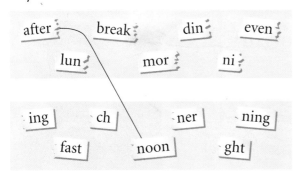

2 Put the times of day in Activity 1 in the table.

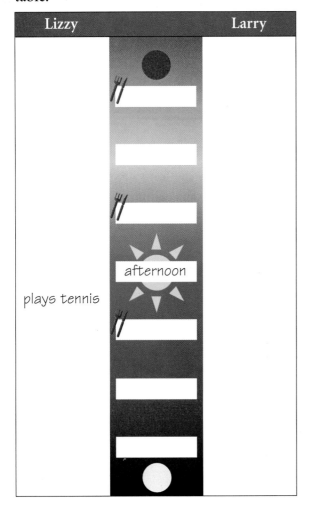

3 Look at the photos on the opposite page. Write these activities by the times of day in Activity 2.

> gets up   goes jogging   goes swimming
> goes to bed   has breakfast   has dinner
> has lunch   listens to music
> paints pictures   plays computer games
> ~~plays tennis~~   reads   watches TV

Sentences

4 Complete these sentences with *Lizzy* or *Larry*.

a On Saturday, _____ gets up at 11.30.

b Before breakfast, _____ goes jogging.

c In the afternoon, _____ listens to music and reads magazines.

d _____ doesn't read before bed, he watches TV.

5 Write four more sentences about Lizzy and Larry. Use *doesn't* in two sentences. Write in your notebook.

Writing

6 Read this paragraph about Lizzy. Then write a paragraph about Larry.

> <u>Saturday with Lizzy</u>
> On Saturday, Lizzy gets up at 7.30. Before breakfast, she goes jogging. For breakfast, she has fruit juice and cereal. In the morning, she paints pictures, writes letters or plays the guitar. After lunch, she swims or plays tennis. Before bed, she doesn't watch TV, she reads a book. She goes to bed at 9.30.

7 Review your writing. Follow this track.

Describing a room

Words

1 Write these words with the pictures.

> bats   beans   fish's head   frog   fruit
> ~~ice~~   key   parrot   pears   sausages
> spider's legs   snake

ice _____   ri _____

_____ ca _____

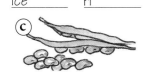
_____ maga _____

_____ eg _____

_____ sand _____

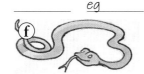
_____ mi _____

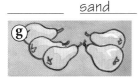
_____ ch _____

_____ bre _____

_____ do _____

_____ bo _____

_____ ca _____

_____ te _____

2 Look at the picture of the Count's kitchen on the opposite page. Find rhyming words. Write the words with the pictures in Activity 1.

ice _____   rice _____

Sentences

3 Complete these sentences about the Count's kitchen.

a There's a _____

b There's some _____

c There are some _____

4 Write sentences with rhymes.

a There's some bread.
   There's a fish's head. _____

b There are some sausages.
   _____

c There's a dog.
   _____

d There's some tea.
   _____

5 Put words in the spaces to finish this rhyme.

There's a carrot and a fish's head,

There's a _____ and there's some

_____ .

Writing

6 Write a poem about the Count and his kitchen. Use these lines at the beginning and again at the end.

> The Count's Kitchen
>
> The Count is a man with a horrible face,
> The Count's kitchen is a terrible place.

7 Review your writing. Follow this track.

17

Giving instructions

Words

1 Label these things.

window _____ _____ _____

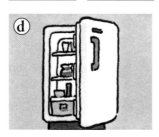

_____ _____ _____ _____

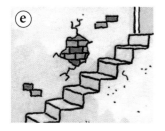

_____ _____ _____ _____

_____ _____ _____ _____

2 Write these verbs below the pictures in Activity 1.

| go down | listen to | look in | open |
| open | sit on | use | watch |

Sentences

3 Look at the picture of the Haunted Holiday Home on the opposite page. Mark these sentences as *good idea* (✓) or *bad idea* (✗).

a Sit on the blue sofa. ✗

b Use the tennis court. _____

c Look in the small mirror. _____

d Use the white telephone. _____

e Open the fridge. _____

f Go down the stairs. _____

g Open the big window. _____

h Watch the TV. _____

i Listen to the radio. _____

4 Change the *bad idea* (✗) sentences. Write in your notebook.

Don't sit on the blue sofa.

5 Write three sentences with one *good idea* and one *bad idea*. Write in your notebook.

Sit on the green sofa, but don't sit on the blue sofa.

Writing

6 Look in the picture of the Haunted Holiday Home. Find a *notice*. Now write the notice. Use this beginning and ending.

> Notice
> Welcome to the Haunted Holiday Home. Enjoy your visit, but be careful!
> • Use the tennis court, but don't use the swimming pool.
> ~~~~~~~~~~~~~~~
> ~~~~~~~~~~~~~~~
> • Finally, <u>never</u> go down the stairs!

7 Review your writing. Follow this track.

Two Bedrooms

Describing where things are

Words

1   Match the things in the room with these words.

☐ bed   ☐ chair   ☐ corner
☐ desk   ☐ door   ☐ floor
☐ shelf   ☐ wall   ☐ wardrobe
☐ window

2   Look at the photos on the opposite page. Write these words in the table.

> ~~bag~~ books   cassettes   football   guitar magazines   paints   pens   posters   shirt skateboard   swimsuit   tennis racket trainers   walkman

Lizzy's room	Larry's room
	bag

Sentences

3   Complete these sentences.

   a   Her _____ are on the wall.

   b   His _____ are on the floor.

   c   Her _____ is in the corner.

   d   His _____ is in the wardrobe.

   e   Her _____ are in a box on her desk.

   f   His _____ is on his bed.

4   Write four more sentences about the rooms. Write in your notebook.

Writing

5   Read this paragraph about Lizzy's room. Then write a paragraph about Larry's room.

> Lizzy's room
> Lizzy's room is very tidy. Her trainers are in the wardrobe and her swimsuit is on the wall. Her books are on the chair. Her pens are in a box on her desk. Her guitar is in the corner. Lizzy can always find her things.

6   Review your writing. Follow this track.

Review Your Writing

UNIT 5

1 Give these pieces of writing a mark for grammar.

good = 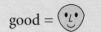 OK = bad =

> On Saturday, Larry get up at 11.30. For breakfast, she have toast and coffee. After breakfast, play computer game.

> On Saturday, Larry get up at 11.30. For breakfast, he has toast and coffee. After breakfast, he plays computer games.

2 Correct the verbs and pronouns.

3 Give your writing a mark for grammar. Are the verbs and pronouns correct?

Finished? Find a watch in the picture on page 14!

UNIT 6

1 Which piece of writing is tidy? Put a
next to this piece of writing.

a
> The Count is a man with a horrible face,
> The Count's kitchen is a terrible place,
> There's a parrot and there's some bread,
> There's a carrot and there's a fish's head.

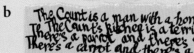

b
>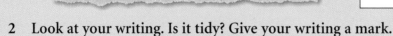
> The Count is a man with a horrible face,
> The The Count's kitchen is a terrible place,
> There's a parrot and there's some bread,
> There's a carrot and there's a fish's head.

2 Look at your writing. Is it tidy? Give your writing a mark.

good = OK = bad =

Finished? Find this shape in the picture on page 16!

UNIT 7

1   Underline the spelling mistakes in this piece of writing.
    How many are there?

> ＊ Use the tenis court, but don't use the swiming pol.
>
> ＊ Sit on the gren sofa, but don't sit on the blue sofa.
>
> ＊ Lok in the smal miror, but don't lok in the big miror.

2   Write one of these comments next to the writing.

   a   Use capital letters at the beginning of sentences!
   b   Be careful with spelling: some words have double letters!
   c   Your spelling is terrible!

3   Check your writing for spelling mistakes.

Finished? Find an insect in the picture on page 18!

UNIT 8

1   Read this piece of writing. There are missing words.
    Write the missing words.

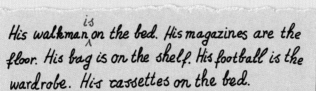

> His walkman _is_ on the bed. His magazines are the
> floor. His bag is on the shelf. His football is the
> wardrobe. His cassettes on the bed.

2   Check your writing. Are there missing words?

Finished? The skateboard and the swimsuit in the pictures
on page 20 are the same colour. True or false?

The Alien of Planet Zeta

Describing appearance and habits

Words

1 Look at the picture on the opposite page. Draw the alien in your notebook.

2 Find words for these parts of the body.

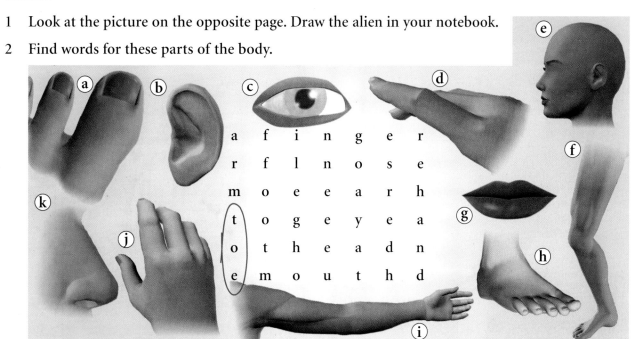

a	f	i	n	g	e	r
r	f	l	n	o	s	e
m	o	e	e	a	r	h
t	o	g	e	y	e	a
o	t	h	e	a	d	n
e	m	o	u	t	h	d

3 Label your picture of the alien. Use two words for each part of the body.

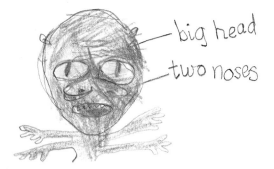

big head

two noses

Sentences

4 Write four more sentences about the alien.

It's got a big head.

It's got two noses.

5 Write two more sentences with *and* or *with*.

It's got two legs and four arms.

It's got a big head with two noses.

Writing

6 Describe the alien. Use these headings:
House, Head, Face, Arms and Legs, Hobbies, Pet.

Begin like this:

The Alien of Planet Zeta
House
There is a house on Planet Zeta. It is the alien's house.
Head

7 Review your writing. Follow this track.

Jane Bond Goes to Seal Island

Telling an adventure story

Words

1 Match these verbs with one or more pictures on the opposite page.

| arrive catch climb drive escape |
| go sleep take |

Picture a _escape, sleep_

Picture b _____

Picture c _____

Picture d _____

Picture e _____

Picture f _____

2 Find eight forms of transport in the pictures. Write the words by the spider's legs.

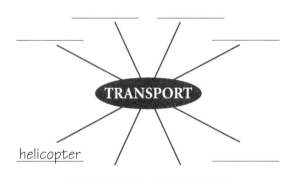

TRANSPORT

helicopter

3 Write the words in Activity 2 in the table.

Air	Land	Water

Sentences

4 Put these words in order to make sentences.

a gun man a catches Jane A with

A man with a gun catches Jane.

b in boat men follow Some a Jane

_____

c Jane of takes rocket the photos

_____

d man The and escapes sleeps Jane

_____

e beach drives boat into gets to a a Jane and

_____

_____

f on Jane climbs arrives island the the rocks and up

_____

_____

5 Write the sentences in Activity 4 again. Change *Jane* to *she* or *her*. Write in your notebook.

a _A man with a gun catches her._

Writing

6 Put the pictures in order and write the story. Use this beginning and ending.

Jane Bond Goes to Seal Island
Jane Bond is a secret agent. In this story, she goes to Seal Island to take photos of a secret rocket.

Finally, she escapes in a helicopter.

7 Review your writing. Follow this track.

Dear Mum and Dad,
    We're having a great time on the school trip. Here's a photo from my hotel room. You can see my friend Lucy. She's sitting at a table in front of the café. She's wearing a red dress.

See you soon!
                    Love from Alex

Identifying friends in a crowd

Words

1 Look at these clothes. Do the puzzle.

1	s				t		
		2	d		r		
		3	g		a		
		4	s		i		
		5	j		n		
		6	s		e		
		7	s		r		
	8	t			s		

2 Find clothes with these colours in the picture on the opposite page. Write a list.

<u>purple</u>   <u>dress</u>

Sentences

3 Give names to these people from the picture.

_____ _____ _____

_____ _____

4 Use your names from Activity 3 to start these sentences.

a _____ is eating an icecream
_____ .

b _____ is riding a bicycle
_____ .

c _____ is skateboarding
_____ .

5 Finish the sentences in Activity 4 with these endings.

between the tree and the telephone
near the fountain
near the fish shop

6 Write sentences for the other two people in Activity 3.

_____

_____

_____

_____

Writing

7 Choose three more friends from the picture. Look at the letter on the opposite page. Write a letter about your three friends.

8 Review your writing. Follow this track.

Describing abilities

Words

1 Write these verbs in the spaces.

> carry clean do play play play post

a _____ bags

b _____ basketball

c _____ letters

d _____ your homework

e _____ games

f _____ shoes

g _____ music

2 Write the phrases in Activity 1 in this table.

Fun	Work

3 Look at these pictures and write more words in the table in Activity 2.

Sentences

4 Complete these sentences.

a A dog is a good friend, but it can't _____ basketball.

b A robodog can play basketball. It can also _____ games, _____ music and _____ your homework!

5 Use these words to make similar sentences.

a dog / good helper / can't / carry bags

_____

_____

b robodog / carry bags / also / and / !

_____

_____

_____

Writing

6 Write an advert for the robodog. Use this beginning and ending.

> Robodog
> Do you want a friend? Do you want a helper? Don't get a dog, get a robodog!
>
> Robodog: a friend at work, a friend at play!

7 Review your writing. Follow this track.

Review Your Writing

1 Give these pieces of writing a mark for handwriting.

good = 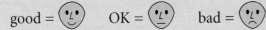 OK =   bad = 😦

> It's got four arm's and two legs.

☐

> It's got a big head with two noses. Its got two leg's and four arms.

☐

2 Correct the apostrophes (').

3 Give your writing a mark for handwriting.
Are the apostrophes correct?

Finished? Find this shape in the picture on page 24!

---

1 Which corrections are tidy: *a* or *b*?

a

> takes photos of the secret rocket. A
> man catch~~es~~ her. The man sleeps
> and ~~**she**~~ escapes.

b

> takes photos of the secret rocket. A
> man catch_e_s her. The man sleeps
> and ~~her~~ she escape_s_.

2 Look at your writing. Are there mistakes? Make tidy
corrections.

Finished? Look at the pictures on page 26. What colour
is Jane's bag?

UNIT 11

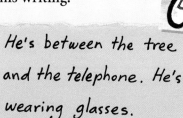

1 Read this piece of writing and look at the picture on page 28. Can you find Martin? Are you sure?

> see my friend Martin. He's in front of the café. He's wearing a green shirt.

You can add more detail to the writing, like this:

> see my friend Martin. He's sitting at a table in front of the café. He's wearing a green shirt, blue jeans and glasses

2 Add more detail to this writing.

> He's between the tree and the telephone. He's wearing glasses.

3 Can you add more detail to your writing?

Finished? How many people in the picture on page 28 have glasses?

UNIT 12

1 Look at the picture on page 30 again. Count the punctuation marks and write the number here.

, = 1   ! = ☐   : = ☐   ' = ☐   ? = ☐

2 Look at these three pieces of writing. Give them a mark for punctuation.

* = no punctuation
** = some punctuation
*** = correct punctuation

3 Give your writing a mark for punctuation.
*, ** or ***

Finished? Look at the picture on page 30. Write the colours of the shopping bags.

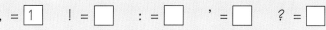

> A dog cant sing. A robopet can sing dance, play the guitar and play games.   ☐

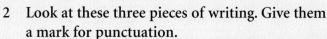

> Do you need a helper Dont get a dog get a robodog A dog Cant dance.   ☐

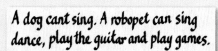

> A dog is a good helper, but it can't clean your shoes. A robodog can clean shoes, cook, carry bags and do your homework!   ☐

Homeland

Bob   Olga   Wendy   Billy

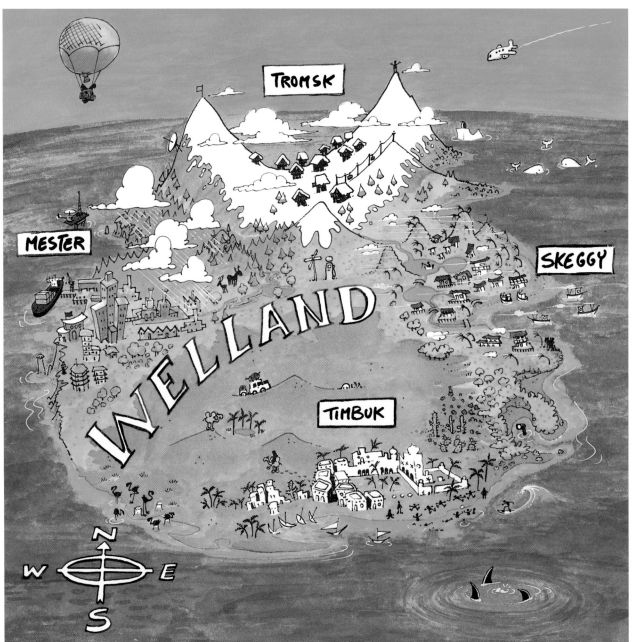

Describing where you live

Words

1 Write these words in the table.

| cloudy cold dry hot rain rainy |
| snow snowy sunny wet windy |

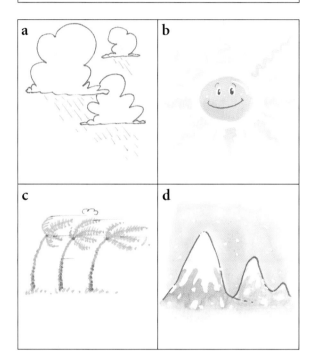

a

b

c

d

2 Look at the map on the opposite page.
Match these words with the places.

| beaches desert forests |
| lakes and rivers mountains |

a north _____
b south _____
c east _____
d west _____

Sentences

3 Write three more sentences about Welland.

There is a desert near Timbuk. _____

_____

_____

_____

4 Write sentences from these notes.

a never rains   It never rains. _____
b always hot   It is always hot. _____
c often snowy + cold

_____

d sometimes windy

_____

e usually sunny + dry

_____

f sometimes cold + wet

_____

g often snows

_____

Writing

5 Read this paragraph. Who wrote it: Billy,
Olga, Bob or Wendy?

I live in Mester. Mester is in the west
of Welland. It is cold and it often rains.
There are forests near Mester. In the
summer holidays, I usually go to Skeggy.
Skeggy is in the east of Welland. There
are lakes and rivers. There are beautiful
beaches, but it is sometimes windy.

Write a similar paragraph for one of the
other people from Welland.

6 Review your writing. Follow this river.

Describing an itinerary

Words

1 Write these words under the pictures.

> barbecue cowboy desert dolphin
> Indian chief pirate riding sheriff
> temple volcano

a _____

b _____

c _____

d _____

e _____

f _____

g _____

h _____

i _____

j _____

Sentences

2 Write sentences from these notes.

a Tomorrow – visit WW

Tomorrow, we're visiting the Wild West.

b First – meet Ind chief

_____

_____

c Then – ride horses with cboys

_____

_____

d After that – have din with s

_____

_____

e Finally – sleep des

_____

_____

Writing

3 You are at Adventure World for two more days. Write a postcard to a friend about it. Use this beginning and ending.

> Dear _____ ,
>
> How are you? We're having a great time at Adventure World. We've got two more days and then we're going home. Tomorrow, ...
>
> Well, that's all the news. See you soon!
>   Love from _____

4 Review your writing. Follow this track.

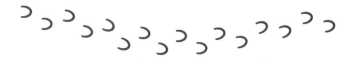

Describing a busy scene

Words

1 Look at the picture on the opposite page.
   Find the animal words in this wordsquare.

```
d  m  p  a  r  r  o  t  c  b
o  o  d  h  o  r  s  e  a  i
l  n  o  s  n  a  k  e  t  r
p  k  g  r  a  b  b  i  t  d
h  e  e  l  e  p  h  a  n  t
i  y  t  o  r  t  o  i  s  e
n  c  r  o  c  o  d  i  l  e
```

2 Label the animals in these pictures. Give
   them names with the same first letter.

_____   _____

_____   _____

_____   Mickey the monkey

Carol the crocodile   _____

Harry the horse   _____

_____   _____

Sentences

3 Finish these sentences with your animal
   names.

   a You can see <u>Mickey the monkey</u> . He's
     going to eat a banana.

   b There on the right you can see _____
     _____ _____ and _____
     _____ _____ . They're going to
     shake hands!

   c In the middle you can see _____
     _____ _____ . She's reading a
     newspaper. Oh no! The ball is going to
     hit her!

   d _____ _____ _____ is
     walking, looking at _____ _____
     _____ . Oh no! He's going to step
     on _____ _____ _____ !

   e _____ _____ _____ and
     _____ _____ _____ are
     going to play table tennis.

4 Write sentences about the other animals.
   Write in your notebook.

─(**Writing**)──────────────────

5 **What does Ricky the rat say? Use this
   beginning and ending.**

   > Hi! I'm Ricky the rat and I'm speaking
   > to you.

   > Oh no! _____ the elephant is
   > going to dive! Run, everybody!

6 Review your writing. Follow this track.

What a Strange Night!

Narrating a story

Words

1 You have got two minutes to add words to this table.

Body	Colours
nose	purple
Animals	Clothes
monkey	shirt

2 Look at the picture on the opposite page and complete these phrases.

a big purple <u>flowers</u>.

b a horrible _____

c a fat _____

d a thin _____

e a yellow and white _____

f a funny _____

g a strange_____

h a small _____

Sentences

3 Add the extra words and write longer sentences.

a There was a snake. (legs long with)
   <u>There was a long snake with legs.</u>

b There was a house. (a mouth and with small purple eyes)

   _____

   _____

c There was a cat. (hat a red with and purple fat trainers)

   _____

   _____

d There was a fish. (yellow umbrella with coat and white blue and a a)

   _____

   _____

   _____

Writing

4 Write a story. Use this beginning and ending.

> <u>What a Strange Night!</u>
> One night, I woke up and I was hungry.
> I went to the kitchen and opened the fridge. In the fridge there was a forest and I walked in.

> I was cold. I opened the door and walked in. I was in my kitchen at home. What a strange night!

5 Review your writing. Follow this track.

Review Your Writing

1 Find four word-order mistakes in this piece of writing.

> There are beaches, but it often is windy.
> In summer, it usually is very hot and it
> rains never, but in winter it sometimes is
> windy. In the summer holidays, I usually
> go to Timbuk in the south of Welland.

Correct the mistakes, like this:

> but it |often| is | windy.

2 Are there any word-order mistakes in your writing?
   Correct the mistakes.

   Finished? Find a submarine in the picture on page 34!

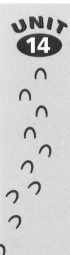

1 Add these words to this piece of writing to make
   time-order clearer for the reader.

   | first   then   after that   finally |

> Tomorrow, we're visiting the Wild West. ^First^ We're
> meeting an Indian chief. We're riding horses
> with cowboys. We're having dinner with the
> sheriff. We're sleeping in the desert.

2 Check your writing. Can you make it clearer for your
   reader?

   Finished? Find a snake in the picture on page 36!

UNIT 15

1 There are four grammar mistakes in this piece of writing. Underline them.

> Terry the tortoise and Polly the parrot is going to playing table tennis. Belinda the bird is going to fly. Rachel the rabbit is playing baseball. Oh no! The ball is going hit Carol the crocodile!

2 Write one of these comments next to the writing.
   a Be careful with *is / are going to*.
   b Check your spelling.

3 Check your writing for grammar mistakes. Give your writing a mark.

Finished? Which of the animals in the picture on page 38 have teeth?

UNIT 16

1 Match the pieces of writing and the comments.

> There were a big green frog with a horrible face.

> I was in my, kitchen at home What a strange night,

> There was a fat cat with a red hat.

> Tere was a funy monkiy. He was eatting blu bananas.

   a Your handwriting is untidy.
   b Be careful with your grammar.
   c Check your spelling.
   d Be careful with your punctuation.

2 Check your writing and write comments. Think about grammar, spelling, punctuation and handwriting.

Finished? How many purple things can you find in the picture on page 40?

Wordlist

Unit 1

creatures
alien
animal
monster
person
robot
other words
friend
from
month
name
old
year

_____

_____

_____

Unit 2

classroom
bag
bin
blackboard
book
chair
computer
desk
door
file
map
notebook
pen
pencil
pencil case
piece of paper
poster
ruler
table
TV
video
wall

_____

_____

_____

Unit 3

family
brother
father
grandfather
grandmother

mother
sister

_____

_____

_____

hobbies
art
football
music
pop magazines
science
swimming

_____

_____

_____

Unit 4

town
bus
café
cinema
disco
hotel
park
post boxes
restaurant
school
shops
sports centre
supermarket
swimming pool
telephone boxes
train
trees

_____

_____

_____

Unit 5

times
at 7.30
in the afternoon
in the evening
in the morning
on Saturday

_____

_____

_____

meals
breakfast
dinner
lunch
activities
get up
go jogging
go swimming
go to bed
have breakfast
listen to music
paint pictures
play computer games
play tennis
read
watch TV

_____

_____

_____

Unit 6

food
beans
bread
carrot
eggs
fish
fruit
ice
milkshake
pears
sandwiches
sausages
tea

_____

_____

_____

animals
bats
cats
dog
frog
mice
parrot
spider

_____

_____

_____

other words
boot
chair
head
key
leg

Unit 7

actions
go down the stairs
listen to the radio
look in the mirror
open the freezer
open the fridge
open the window
sit on the sofa
use the telephone
house
basement
tennis court
other words
big
black
blue
green
small
white

———————

———————

———————

Unit 8

house
bed
chair
corner
desk
door
floor
shelf
wall
wardrobe
window

———————

———————

———————

other words
bag
cassettes
football
guitar
shirt

skateboard
swimsuit
tennis racket
trainers
walkman

———————

———————

———————

Unit 9

body
arm
ear
eye
finger
foot
hand
head
leg
mouth
nose
toe

———————

———————

———————

activities
drive a car
play basketball
play the guitar
ride a bicycle

———————

———————

———————

other words
alien
dog
hobby
house
planet
with

Unit 10

transport
bicycle
boat
bus
car
helicopter
plane
rocket
ship

———————

———————

———————

activities
arrive
catch
climb
escape
follow
fall asleep
take

———————

———————

———————

other words
beach
film
gun
island
rocks
secret agent

Unit 11

clothes
dress
jeans
shirt
shoes
shorts
skirt
trousers

———————

———————

———————

colours
black
blue
brown
green
orange
purple
red
white
yellow

———————

———————

———————

other words
fountain
friend
glasses
icecream
trip

Unit 12

fun
basketball
games
sing
swim

_____

_____

_____

work
carry bags
clean
cook
homework
post letters
shop
wash up

_____

_____

_____

other words
also
clothes
helper
want

Unit 13

weather
hot
cold
dry
wet
cloudy
rainy
snowy
sunny
windy

_____

_____

_____

directions
north
south
east
west

countryside
beaches
desert
forests
lakes
mountains
rivers

_____

_____

_____

other words
never
sometimes
often
usually
always

Unit 14

people
cowboy
Indian chief
pirate
sheriff

_____

_____

_____

time words
first
then
after that
finally

other words
barbecue
temple
volcano

Unit 15

animals
bird
cat
crocodile
dog
dolphin
elephant
horse
monkey

parrot
rabbit
snake
tortoise

_____

_____

_____

activities
eat
play
read
shake hands
walk

_____

_____

_____

Unit 16

colours
purple

_____

_____

_____

body
nose

_____

_____

_____

animals
monkey

_____

_____

_____

clothes
shirt

_____

_____

_____

other words
big
fat
funny
horrible
small
strange
thin

Student Record Sheet

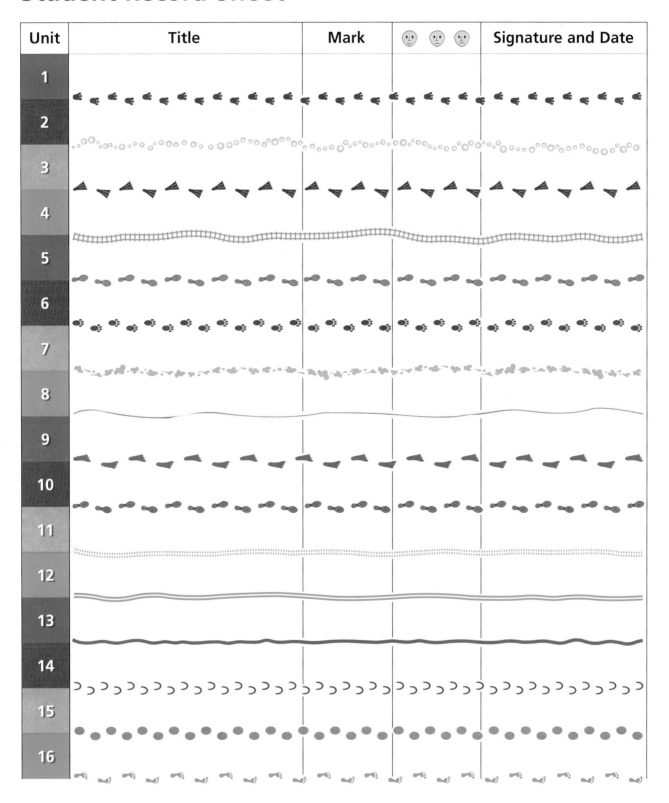

Unit	Title	Mark	😊 😐 ☹	Signature and Date
1				
2				
3				
4				
5				
6				
7				
8				
9				
10				
11				
12				
13				
14				
15				
16				

OXFORD
UNIVERSITY PRESS

Great Clarendon Street, Oxford OX2 6DP

Oxford University Press is a department of the University of Oxford. It furthers the University's objective of excellence in research, scholarship, and education by publishing worldwide in

Oxford New York

Athens Auckland Bangkok Bogotá Buenos Aires Calcutta Cape Town Chennai Dar es Salaam Delhi Florence Hong Kong Istanbul Karachi Kuala Lumpur Madrid Melbourne Mexico City Mumbai Nairobi Paris São Paulo Singapore Taipei Tokyo Toronto Warsaw

with associated companies in Berlin Ibadan

Oxford and Oxford English are registered trade marks of Oxford University Press in the UK and in certain other countries

ISBN 019433202 0

1999 Impression

Printed in Hong Kong

Acknowledgements

The authors would like to thank the teachers and students in Greece, Spain and Turkey who reviewed and trialled Pen Pictures. Their feedback was invaluable in shaping the course.

In addition, the authors would like to give special thanks to Amanda Hancock for her generous help and professional insight.

Illustrations by: James Browne pp. 34, 35, 42; Stephen Dell p.30, 33; Emma Dodd pp. 31, 41; Robin Edmonds pp. 4, 5, 12, 18, 19, 23; Jonathan Hateley pp. 6, 7, 12; Kev Hopgood pp. 10, 11, 13, 24, 25, 32; Phillip Reeve pp. 8, 9, 13, 28, 29, 33; Peter Seal p. 21; Ron Tiner pp. 16, 17, 22, 40, 43; Chris West pp. 26, 32, 36, 37, 42; David Woodward pp. 38, 39, 43
Handwriting throughout and alien illustration p. 25 by Kathy Baxendale

Cover illustration by: Jonathan Hateley

Commissioned photography by: Bill Osment

With additional thanks to: Marston Ferry Sports Centre, Oxford